# CALIFORNIA DREAMING

Photographic prints are available.
Visit the website: richardblair.com,
or email richard@richardblair.com.

Color & Light Editions
P. O. Box 934
Point Reyes Station, CA 94956
415 663-1616

EASTSDE BROOK
*Bishop, Owens Valley*

Richard Blair
*photographer, book designer, author*
Kathleen P. Goodwin
*editor, foreword*

# CALIFORNIA DREAMING

Photographs by
## RICHARD BLAIR

COLOR & LIGHT EDITIONS
Inverness, California

FOR KATHLEEN

FALL, McGee Creek

*Inyo National Forest*

# FOREWORD

*California Dreaming* was photographed over many years. I was there when quite a few of these photographs were taken. The one common element of each experience was the excitement of the moment, the feeling of discovery.

Many of the images were shot with view cameras that used 4 x 5 or 8 x 10 inch film, set up on a tripod and carefully composed. Sometimes it was a leisurely process, other times speed was essential. I remember when the picture on the cover of *California Dreaming* was taken. The mist in Yosemite Valley was exquisite and Blair captured it on film. Five minutes later a class of enthusiastic photographers arrived, armed with all manner of equipment, but the moment was gone. The valley was still beautiful, the magic had disappeared.

When we are all packed up ready to start a trip, people sometimes ask where we were heading. "To the eastside or down the coast," we reply vaguely—and that is the beginning of our adventure. More often than not, we do not have a specific plan or even a date when we have to return. We have woken up in wonderful places. Our ideal way is to be lying on our foam pad, out in the open, with the sky overhead and no other person in miles. The day seems full of promise. The dawn chorus of birds is in full swing, the sun's rays are edging towards our sleeping bags and we are torn between recording the sunrise or staying warm.

With his eye for beauty and form, and well-honed technical expertise, Blair has assembled a remarkable collection of images. Using photography, graphic design and printing, he has been able to create books with his vision. By doing so many of the jobs himself to produce his books, he achieves a clarity of purpose and a quality which is maintained from lens to printed page.

I hope *California Dreaming* is an inspiration to all. Go out and experience these places of California. Take the extra steps often required to see something extraordinary.

*We'll be there in spirit . . .*

-Kathleen Goodwin
*Inverness, California*

HOG ISLAND, SUN AND FOG

*Tomales Bay*

# PREFACE

This book is a homage to the great landscape photographers in the f/64 tradition. Edward Weston and Ansel Adams are the gods of this group.

What were they doing? What were their goals? Finding a scene, wonderful in form and detail, then photographing it with the sharpest, most revealing cameras, optics and film. Printing was equally disciplined. Hours were spent in the darkroom, using mysterious, proprietary and probably toxic developers, combined with marathon sessions of contact printing or enlarging, trying to remember complex burning and dodging strategies. All this work produced prints that glowed with a luminous, radioactive intensity. There were many chemical baths; to tone, color, add depth to the black tones, and to protect the prints from aging. Not-so-kosher techniques—waxing the surface of prints with shoe wax, and painting bird wings on black spots in the sky—were also employed. These wonderful darkroom skills are being lost. Digital printing is taking over, and darkrooms are now darker than ever.

It was a great run. The f/64ers were to photography, as the Impressionists were to painting, because they set a new direction for nature photographers. They rejected the conventional soft-focus Pictorialism, popular in the early 1930s. Their name came from the large-format camera's smallest aperture setting, which ensures great depth of field. They encouraged each other, competing with gusto, while the world convulsed with the Great Depression and the increasing rumbles of a new war. The formal group only lasted two years but its members continued to be influential. World War II, the Holocaust, and the mean streets of urban America were skillfully depicted by photojournalists working for Life and Look. These photographs showed a world of nightmares in sharp focus.

Wandering around California, looking for dramatic, perfect scenes, without any visible human influence is a joy for me. It is not unlike finding a bower in the woods, the perfect place to lie with a lover, or the joy of being atop a mountain in moonlight, watching the shadows of clouds slide across the trees below. It's not an accurate depiction of life, it's a dream I have, we all have, to live in those peak moments.

These romantic, perfect views are not the full story. Look, I know that the world is going to hell with global warming, pollution and overpopulation. The human race's many sins may doom us to a lousy future. Where does the f/64 group's philosophy fit into this new reality?

I could photograph tract housing, bad architecture, freeways, and say that this is California. Well I do photograph these scenes. They are California. However, it is equally valid to find perfect nature scenes. We need hope—hope in large amounts now. When I was younger, the Sierra Club seemed to offer hope that wilderness could be saved. Then we all realized that there was a bigger problem, that of saving the world from the transgressions of global resource depletion. This can lead to despair.

But we still have to go into the mystic. These natural places still exist. They are hard to get to, but it's not that difficult. Find some wilderness, not the wilderness of Lewis and Clark, or later, the wilderness of John Muir, but find the wilderness of your imagination. It may be a dream, but without it, life is a lot bleaker.

My wife, Kathleen Goodwin, and I, have had incredible adventures visiting these photographic sites over the past forty years. We camped out, carrying everything ourselves (a big mistake), drove like hell, and took the pain with the pleasure. She sure made the journey wonderful, and she still does.

Remember back in grade school, what did you write for your school essay? Was it My Summer Vacation? Why not revive your childhood? Find havens, tiny and grand, to come back to until you are at home on the earth.

-Richard Blair
Inverness, California

BURNEY FALLS
*Modoc County*

# TABLE OF CONTENTS

RE-INTRODUCED CALIFORNIA CONDOR
*Big Sur*

TURKEY VULTURE AND PINE

*Pinnacles National Monument*

# INTRODUCTION

California wilderness is now a fantasy. However, dreaming of wilderness can help

preserve it. While we can never have the experience of early explorers who saw these

lands unaltered, the idea of parks—land set aside for the enjoyment of all—allows us

to imagine ourselves as part of nature, with pristine landscapes and viable habitats.

It's a dream to believe in.

Half Dome from Olmsted Point

# YOSEMITE AND THE SIERRA

No temple made with hands can compare with Yosemite. Every rock in its walls seems to glow with life...

Awful in stern, immovable majesty, how softly these rocks are adorned, and how fine and reassuring the company they keep: Their feet among beautiful groves and meadows, their brows in the sky, a thousand flowers leaning confidingly against their feet, bathed in floods of water, floods of light...

– *John Muir*

HALF DOME, RISING MOON

(THANKS, ANSEL)

Yosemite Valley after Spring Rain
*Yosemite National Park*

DAY-OLD FAWN

*near Echo Lake, Yosemite National Park*

BLACK BEAR

*near Glacier Point, Yosemite National Park*

EL CAPITAN, WINTER
*Yosemite National Park*

SNOW PILLOWS, MERCED RIVER
*Yosemite Valley*

Clouds and Snow, Sentinel Rock
*Yosemite Valley*

John Muir's Cabin Site, Lower Yosemite Falls
*Yosemite Valley*

Merced River and Cathedral Cliffs
*from the El Capitan Bridge, Yosemite Valley*

Meandering Merced River in Yosemite Valley
*from the Diving Board, Half Dome*

HALF DOME FROM THE DIVING BOARD
*Yosemite National Park*

MERCED RIVER IN WINTER
*Yosemite National Park*

Yosemite Falls in Winter, with a Snow Cone

*Yosemite Valley*

Spring Food, Happy Isles

*Yosemite Valley*

MERCED RIVER AT EL PORTAL, SPRING

*Yosemite National Park*

ROYAL ARCH CASCADE

*Yosemite Valley*

Chilnualna Falls

*Wawona, Yosemite National Park*

UPPER YOSEMITE FALLS
*Columbia Point, Yosemite Valley*

30

HALF DOME WITH THUNDERHEAD
*from Glacier Point, Yosemite Valley*

BRIDALVEIL FALLS AND
LEANING TOWER, SPRING
*Yosemite Valley*

BRIDALVEIL CREEK, BELOW THE FALLS
*Yosemite Valley*

BRIDALVEIL FALLS, WINTER
*Yosemite Valley*

Black Oak and Cathedral Cliffs, Fall
*Yosemite Valley*

Black Oak and Cathedral Cliffs, Winter
*Yosemite Valley*

Unicorn Peak

Tresidder Peak

Cathedral Peak

Cathedral Peak from Lower Cathedral Lake
*Yosemite National Park*

ROCK GARDEN, LOWER CATHEDRAL LAKE
*Yosemite National Park*

DETAIL OF CLIMBERS

CLIMBERS, PYWIACK DOME
*Yosemite National Park*

SNAG, LOWER CATHEDRAL LAKE
*Yosemite National Park*

Fallen Log, Lyell Creek
*Yosemite National Park*

ICEFALL, WEST OF
LEANING TOWER
*Yosemite Valley*

43

Mount Dana and Mount Gibbs from Dana Fork, Tuolumne River

*Yosemite National Park*

TUFA FORMATION
*Mono Lake*

Bud Lake and Cathedral Peak

*Yosemite National Park*

Minarets from Lake Ediza
*Ansel Adams Wilderness, Inyo National Forest*

REDWOODS
*Sequoia-Kings Canyon National Park*

Merced River, Bunnell Cascade

*Yosemite National Park*

The Southern Sierra from the Alabama Hills

*Inyo National Forest*

MINARETS WITH THUNDERHEADS

*Inyo National Forest*

EMERALD BAY, LAKE TAHOE

*Emerald Bay State Park*

Point Reyes Headlands and Drakes Bay

*Point Reyes National Seashore*

# THE PACIFIC SHORE

Pristine beaches, wild waves

Jumbled mountains offering dramatic evidence of past upheavals

Waterfalls dropping precipitously into the ocean

Glorious marine life

Primeval redwoods

Space to breathe.

-Kathleen Goodwin

Condor Soaring over Big Sur

PFEIFFER BEACH (BOTH)
*JULIA PFEIFFER BURNS STATE PARK, BIG SUR*

McWay Falls, Julia Pfeiffer Burns State Park

*Big Sur*

GARRAPATA STATE PARK

*Big Sur*

DRAKES BEACH PANORAMA

*Point Reyes National Seashore*

McClures Beach

*Point Reyes National Seashore*

CLAYTON AND JOE CAST THE NET
*Tomales Bay*

Fishing Boats and Kent Island, Outgoing Tide
*Bolinas Lagoon*

Drakes Beach
*Point Reyes National Seashore*

DOUGLAS FIRS IN FOG, INVERNESS RIDGE

*Fire Lane Trail, Point Reyes National Seashore*

ROCK, SEA, SAND
*Point Reyes National Seashore*

BEACHCOMBER SHELTER, KEHOE BEACH (LOOKING NORTH)
*Point Reyes National Seashore*

BEACHCOMBER SHELTER, KEHOE BEACH (LOOKING SOUTH)

*Point Reyes National Seashore*

Cabin in the Fog

*Sonoma County*

Snow by Moonlight (with the Lighthouse on the Farallones)
*Inverness Ridge, Marin*

LICHEN ON BAY TREES,
OLEMA VALLEY
*Point Reyes National Seashore*

FERN CANYON
*Prairie Creek Redwoods
State Park*

SCULPTURED BEACH

*Point Reyes National Seashore*

DRAKES BEACH

*Point Reyes National Seashore*

OYSTERMAN AT JOHNSON'S OYSTERS
*Drakes Estero, Point Reyes National Seashore*

Point Reyes Headlands and Drakes Bay
*from Chimney Rock Trail*

Point Bonita Lighthouse and the Golden Gate

Starfish and Rock Formation
*Sculptured Beach*

TREES AT DIVIDE MEADOW

*Point Reyes*

Papermill Creek in Dappled Sun

*Samuel P. Taylor State Park*

Overhanging Branches

*Bolinas Ridge Trail, Marin*

The Slopes of Mount Tamalpais

ROCK, TREE, BLACKBIRDS
*Petaluma, California*

Cow and Big Oak (now suburbia)

*Lucas Valley, Marin County*

EEL GRASS

*Tomales Bay*

PIGEON POINT LIGHTHOUSE
*Pescadero, California*

TREES IN THE FOG
*Road to Dillon Beach*

REDWOODS AND
STREAM BANK
*Muir Woods*

KIDD CREEK
*Cazadero*

Papermill Creek
*Samuel P. Taylor State Park*

EUREKA DUNES

*Death Valley National Park*

# CALIFORNIA DESERTS

All the aspects of this desert are beautiful, whether you behold it in fair weather or foul, or when the sun is just breaking out after a storm, and shining on its moist surface in the distance, it is so white, and pure, and level...

*-Henry David Thoreau*

JOSHUA TREES
*Joshua Tree National Park*

View From Zabriskie Point
*Death Valley National Park*

Broken Salt Flats
*Death Valley National Park*

Natural Bridge
*Death Valley National Park*

UBEHEBE CRATER

*Death Valley National Park*

Corkscrew Canyon, from Zabriskie Point
*Death Valley National Park*

THE RACETRACK

*Death Valley National Park*

The Grandstand in the Racetrack
*Death Valley National Park*

Salt Snake, Saline Valley

*Death Valley National Park*

IN SALINE VALLEY

*Death Valley National Park*

EUREKA DUNES

*Death Valley National Park*

BADWATER

*Death Valley National Park*

SALT SPRING HILL AND AVAWATZ MOUNTAINS
*Death Valley National Park*

Trucks Marching across the Desert

*Highway 40, Mojave Desert*

Dante's View

*Death Valley National Park*

Panorama from Aguereberry Point

*Death Valley National Park*

MIDDLE ALKALI LAKE
*Surprise Valley, Modoc County*

Salt Pan and Panamint Range

*Death Valley National Park*

Furnace Creek Wash and Twenty Mule Team Canyon
*Death Valley National Park*

WILD BURROS
*Owlshead Mountains, Death Valley National Park*

WHITE PELICANS
*Salton Sea*

ROCK MELANGE, TITUS CANYON
*Death Valley National Park*

MOJAVE RATTLESNAKE
*Mojave National Preserve*

YUCCA FLOWERS AND FRONDS
*Joshua Tree National Park*

YUCCA FRONDS
*Mojave National Preserve*

JOSHUA TREE DESERT SCENE

JOSHUA TREE SILHOUETTES
*Joshua Tree National Park*

JOSHUA TREE FLOWER
*Joshua Tree National Park*

PINNACLES NATIONAL MONUMENT

Aeromotor Windmill

# RELICS AND RUINS

"A land without ruins is a land without memories;

a land without memories is a land without history."

*-Abram Joseph Ryan*

Wagon Wheels from the Twenty Mule Team
*Death Valley National Park*

SADDLE, HOME RANCH
*Point Reyes National Park*

DEER SCULL, HOME RANCH
*Point Reyes National Park*

BODIE

*Bodie State Historic Park*

Dechambeau Hotel and I.O.O.F. Building (Independent Order of Odd Fellows)
*Bodie State Historic Park*

Bed Frame and Old Sock

*Bodie State Historic Park*

KITCHEN TABLE

*Bodie State Historic Park*

DOOR WITH CURTAIN
*Bodie State Historic Park*

FISHING BOAT TOSSED UP BY STORM
*Orick, Humboldt County*

Wreck of the Point Reyes

*Inverness*

PETE AGUEREBERRY'S BUICK
*Death Valley National Park*

FORD PICKUP

*Black Diamond Hills State Park*

1953 BUICK EIGHT AND FRIEND
*Half Moon Bay*

Car Roof, Owlshead Canyon
*Death Valley*

ANCHOR MADE FROM RIM, LAIRD'S LANDING

*Tomales Bay*

Sausalito Houseboats, 1975
*Sausalito*

BATHTUB AND DOOR
*Sonoma County*

Swing in Fog
*Sonoma County*

View from Abandoned Car, Alkali Lake

*Modoc County*

TACK ROOM WINDOW, HOME RANCH

*Point Reyes National Seashore*

INSTITUTE OF GEOPHYSICS AND PLANETARY PHYSICS, SYSTEMWIDE OFFICES
*Ozone, California*

# Photographer's Notes

The world is changing fast for photographers. Ten years ago, I started down the path to digital imaging using a drum scanner for film images. Since I've been a photographer for over forty years, the bulk of my photographs have been shot on film. There are only twenty images shot with a digital camera in this book. While I mean to use my film cameras, notably the 8 x 10 view camera, I find it very hard to go back.

Like everyone else, I like the instant feedback of using a computer screen to edit positives and also the ability to show everyone my images via the web. However, as someone with many years' experience in the darkroom and the ability to do museum-quality prints, it is incumbent upon me to continue in the old tradition to satisfy collectors who want silver-gelatin prints. They represent the end of an amazing era. Darkroom prints will become a rarity soon. If silver-gelatin prints are properly done, they are hard to equal for beauty. Digital prints do have many advantages, like unlimited burning and dodging, spot and scratch removal, easy toning, and a simple path to archival permanence. Nowadays I probably make ten times as many pigment (inkjet) prints as darkroom prints. But silver-gelatin prints really have magical qualities. Just seeing the ghostly latent image come up in the developer tray is sorcery indeed.

The most important factors in taking landscapes is the photographer's skill, the subject, and the conditions of light. For me, it matters little if the camera is digital or film. Light is still light. Framing, details, point of view, time–it's all the same.

People have more confidence that digital images will work for their needs, rather than waiting for an image on film to get developed. There was alchemy in that process, but actually, there's more magic in shooting a picture, and e-mailing immediately. It is amazing to me that people anywhere in the world can see pictures on my website.

My response to digital imaging was to broaden my skills to include graphic design and publishing, both areas in the arts with steep learning curves. That effort has produced this book and six others. My first book, *Point Reyes Visions*, was done in 1998 when computers were barely able to handle making a large color book. I love pre-visualizing a book, writing it, and designing it. Typography, book design, book binding, paper selection, and the smell of lithographic ink are all great joys to me. I learned about printing in the pre-digital age when I worked as a lithographic cameraman and stripper, turning artwork into composite films to burn plates. My studio, Color & Light, was unusual because in addition to doing photography projects, we also could also make films that printers could print from on their presses. We created duotone photographs, in which two colors are used to add drama and suble color tones to images by double printing them. (This book is printed with black and grey duotones). It was good training for book projects! When the medium is ink on paper, painterly skills like varnishing and spot colors are added to the photographer's palette.

Still, I encourage readers who want to see these images as fine art prints to do so. At large sizes the prints are more evocative of place; that quality which gives you the illusion of being there. You can learn about upcoming shows via my website, richardblair.com. It's a resource for seeing my other photographic subjects. My working facilities are open to the public as part of Point Reyes Open Studios.

Please enjoy my work. I hope it inspires you to dream about California's glorious, primal past, while enjoying the places that still have incredible beauty. Work to conserve their wildness, improve animal habitats and, at least for me, preserve the views!

-Richard Blair
Inverness, California
Summer, 2011

Cow Contemplating The Void
*Point Reyes*

Offset Lithography Press, Al Jones Litho, San Francisco
*The first press Richard Blair made plates for, and the machine which printed his first lithograph.*

# COLOR & LIGHT EDITIONS

## Celebrating California's wild places & cultural innovations since the sixties

### Visions of Marin

Text and Photography by Richard Blair and Kathleen Goodwin
240 color pages, 420 photographs 9" x 12"

The editor of the *Pacific Sun*, Jason Walsh, called **Visions of Marin** "the most quintessentially Marin entry in a series of publications that are becoming the definitive visual history of the county." hardbound, ISBN 978-0-9671527-5-2 **$39.95**

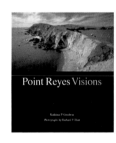

### Point Reyes Visions: a Bay Area best seller!

Text and Photography by Richard Blair and Kathleen Goodwin
192 color pages, 256 photographs, 9" x 11"

"The photos not only capture the place, but are like windows looking at past adventures. Sections on adjacent Tomales Bay and Mount Tamalpais are a bonus to the jewel-quality photos of the Bay Area's favorite national park." - Tom Stienstra, Outdoor Columnist, *San Francisco Chronicle*
clothbound ISBN 0-9671527-4-7 **$45.00** black cover

### California Trip

Text and Photography by Richard Blair and Kathleen Goodwin
300 color pages, 600 photographs, 11" x 11" Gold medal winner: best non-fiction regional book, west coast.- *Independent Book Publishers Award*

"Plunk the entire state down on your coffee table in the breathtakingly beautiful '**California Trip**' ... this book should be on every California coffee table" - Patricia Lynn Henley, *North Bay Bohemian*
clothbound, ISBN 0-9671527-3-9 **$29.95** (new price) choice of cover jackets

### Point Reyes Visions Guidebook

Text and Photography by Richard Blair and Kathleen Goodwin
80 B&W pages, 62 duotone photographs, 5" x 7"

"The slim, 80 page book, which slips easily into a backpack, features stunning photographs of Point Reyes sites as well as factual information and basic directions for potential visitors. It includes a handy foldout map. With it's high quality photos and design, the **Point Reyes Visions Guidebook** is ideal for casual adventurers who also want a nice keepsake." - Kristin Bartus, *Pacific Sun*
clothbound ISBN 0-9671527-0-4 **$14.99**

To order our books, acquire photographic prints, or join our mailing list, please call or email:

415 663-1616
richard@richardblair.com

Online ordering:
richardblair.com

COLOR & LIGHT EDITIONS
P.O.Box 934
Point Reyes, CA 94956

Pine needles floating in a Sierra lake, lit by the morning sun

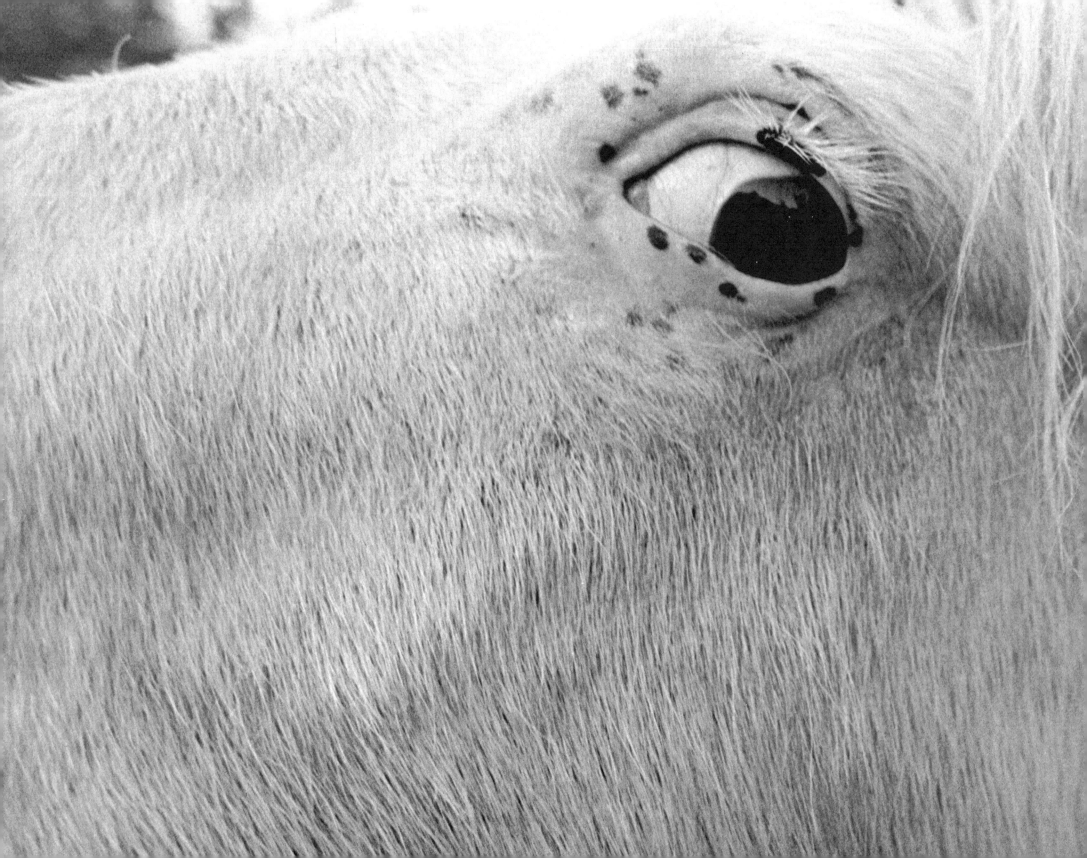